THE LANDSCAPE DEEPER IN

BOOKS BY THE SAME AUTHOR

Poetry

Common Places
Weedpatch or Jericho?
The Arafura Sea
The Perfect Country of Words
Eye

Other

Dear Viola: Reporting, Writing and Editing
for the Student Journalist
Under the Heaven Tree: An Indiana Childhood

Some poems in this volume appeared earlier in: *Plains Poetry Journal, Beloit Poetry Journal, Kentucky Poetry Review, Passages North, Apogee, Roanoke Review, Poet Lore, Literally, Riverrun, Flying Island, Hopewell Review, Vigilance, Ant Poetry, Mankato Poetry Review,* and the website of *Poets Against the War.* Several also appeared in *Eye*, published by Pleasure Boat Studio, and in the four other chapbooks listed above.

"The Landscape Deeper In," by William Bridges. ISBN 978-1-58939-712-5.

Published 2005 by Virtualbookworm.com Publishing Inc., P.O. Box 9949, College Station, TX 77842, US. ©2005, William Bridges. All rights reserved. No part of this publication may be reproduced, stored in a retrieval system, or transmitted in any form or by any means, electronic, mechanical, recording or otherwise, without the prior written permission of William Bridges.

Manufactured in the United States of America.

the Landscape Deeper In

Selected Poems, 1974-2004
by William Bridges

TO MY WIFE,
KAREN PETERSEN BRIDGES

Note on stanza breaks: In most cases, the point at which a poem carries over to another page is also a stanza break. The exceptions occur at the bottom of pages 12, 32, 60, 82, 123, 124, and 132.

Cover: The cover photo, by the author, is a view from Village Bay toward Hirte, the main island of the St. Kilda archipelago, a group of Scottish islands in the North Atlantic. (However, for layout reasons, the image has been reversed.)

COVER TYPOGRAPHY: LINDSAY HADLEY

CONTENTS
I
WOODS DOOR 1
DESIGN 2
LAND'S END 3
VENICE: SUNDAY MORNING IN THE GESUATI 4
ON THE K & I BRIDGE 5
THE MILL 6
OLD ELLERMAN 8
MORNING 9
AMERICAN ARCHAEOLOGY 10
THE SHIPYARD 12
ON THE DIFFICULTY OF CHANGING ANYTHING 14
A CHILD'S SONG OF SPACE 15
STILL-LIFE WITH MYSTERY 16
II
A PROBLEM OF ART 17
! 18
THE CONQUEST OF SPACE 19
61 DEGREES NORTH 20
HOLY CROSS CITY 21
PASSAGE 22
METAPHOR 23
THE DREAM OF BOY BLUE 24
HARDTACK'S VERANDAH 26
WHAT THE DEAD ARE TRYING TO TELL US 28
THE MOVEMENT 29
VANDERHOOF'S ETCHING 30
THE WATER WITCH 32

ON THE ROUTE IN AUGUST 34
UPSTATE DAYS 37
WITH TIME 38
BELIEVERS 39
THE STORM 42
THE TREE NEXT DOOR 44

III

EYE 45
THE SCHOOLROOM 46
THE IDEA OF DOMINION 48
PHRASE FROM A LETTER 51
THE DARK 52
MY WIFE DANCES WITH OUR SONS 53
QUARRELING THROUGH THE LOUVRE 54
ASH LIMBS 56
WHAT WE DID IN JULY 58
THE BIRDS & ME 59
GOING UNDER THE HOUSE 60
CATCHES 62
WITNESS 63
TO A WRITER WHO HASN'T WRITTEN YET 64
THE SOLDIERS 65
AND SUDDENLY FLOWERS 68
ONE OF THE DEATHS 69
WHAT REALLY WAS 70
THE MANSIONS ON SOUTH THIRD 71
NARRATIVE 72
FOR SALLY IN HAWAII 74

IV

THE ARAFURA SEA 75
THE SENEGALESE PHOTOS IN MONTREAL 79

AT THE HOUSE OF NIYAMÓYOANA YABAI 80
THE WORLD AS IT IS 81
FROM A CHEAP HOTEL AT EDGE OF KNOWN WORLD .. 82
THE AIKIDO MASTER 84
BRONZE 86
TAIPEI MOTORSCOOTER LOVE POEM 88
LITTLE CHINESE POEM 89
BASHO & LANDSCAPE 90
GODS, MEN, AND TIGERS 92
IN THE TIME OF THE YELLOW EMPEROR 93
RETURNING TO TAIPEI 94
THE PHOTOGRAPHS OF MARTIN CHAMBI 95
WINE TREE 96
HELLABRUN 97
THE TIN SINGERS 98
THE TINSMITH WHO BECAME A MIME 99
AN IRISH SALTSPOON 100

V

ARTIFACTS 101
WHAT WAS PASSING 102
SNOWMELT 103
TWO STORIES 104
SCHOLAR AND SEAGULL 105
WALKING WITH FRIENDS IN OLD-GROWTH FOREST .. 106
THE LANDSCAPE DEEPER IN 108
WRITING A POEM 109
LETTER TO PORT TOWNSEND 110
MESSAGES 112
THE NEW YORK GIRL 113
ALL THAT DIVIDES 114
IN THE MALL 115

GODDESS & MUSE 116
LINES FOR A LUMINOUS DIAL 117
INVITATION TO A GHOST 118
DESCARTES AND THE ANGEL 120
SILKBY TO KELBY 122

VI

NOTES FROM THE ISLAND 123
UNTITLED 128
RED GLADS, BLUE MOUNTAIN 129
PONIES 130
LETTER FROM INDIANA 131
BERLIN REVISITED 132
NEAR GOSHEN 134
SOME DREAMS 135
AN IMPERFECT SONNET 136
MARTIAN MOMENT 137
PYRUS COMMUNIS 138
A MOUNTAIN THINKS 140
ALL-POINTS BULLETIN 141
SALVATION 142
EPITHALAMIUM 144
MACROMICROCOSMIC 145
YOUR BENCH 146

I

WOODS DOOR

I'd slipped my mother's survey,
most careless of sons;
I was too new to say
if I was anyone's.

The path, if path, by the husk
of a winter-killed row
led on into a dusk
(of trees, I'd say now).

But trees had been few before,
and it seemed little odd
there should be the shape of a door
and coiled stones in the sod.

In the last yellow light
of a child's long day,
something held me that wasn't fright
before I was called away.

But it left me changed in the mind,
and ever since then
I've half expected to find
a door in a woods again.

DESIGN

Notes without signature
in the roads blow;
wind's fingers trace a pure
calligraphy of snow.

On macadam slates, white
sentences uncoil;
quills of air, quick, slight,
write and then spoil.

Parabolas of meaning
curve at us, but veer;
in the wind's keening,
no voice is clear.

Snowfall to storm grown
covers all design—
O, but for a moment shown
the curve, the line.

LAND'S END

Where the land ends, the dock wades out
on stilts, as far as it can,
a few poles and planks,
crooked as the Malay Peninsula,
last print on the dark river.

At the end it is hardly more
than a reflection.
Only very small brown feet
could run all the way out,
only small brown hands
let down a coil of fine line
into those waters.

One thinks of ends,
last rocks and selvages, the skerry
beyond the last island in a chain,
French Frigate Shoal,
skirl in the water,

the continents pared down
to a foothold,
last purchase of earth,
telling us what earth is.

VENICE: SUNDAY MORNING IN THE GESUATI

An old woman kisses God's toe and goes out.
Bees drip from the mouth of a priest.
Tiepolo's angels are flying somewhere
above the scaffolding, but spring
has come in from the Zattere.
A freighter is moving up the channel.
Coffee is being served at Nico's.

Three girls lean over the organ case to flirt
with the young organist. God hears
antiphonal laughter. He is here
in the person of an old priest
who has been walking under the trees
by San Agnese and has come in
to rest his feet. The girls please him.

They rise up the side aisle afterward,
momentary angels, graceful and smiling,
stooping to hug a solemn, dressed-up child.
Their love this morning is enough to cover
organists, little boys, even God.
They bob to Him, lord of the year,
who blesses and sends their blitheness into spring.

ON THE K & I BRIDGE

One moment only the rusted trestle, then
as though loosed by a thrilling of the rail,
bright showers of birds are spilled upon the air
like coins from a cut purse, fish turned from a creel.

Sudden wealth! Who could have imagined it?
This silver milling, echelons of wings
that wheel and storm the fastness of the bridge
in staggering rush against the weight of things,

then fall away, descending into steel
and quickening it, like water into sand,
or soul re-entering body. Where they flew,
the sly recoverings of a miser's hand.

THE MILL

Down in the ancient belly of the mill
in a long age of axle grease and flour,
the diesel fired, a shaft took up the slack
in forty belts put surely under power.
Some broad as elephants, some nearly strings,
running on wheels with cams of precise quirk,
they flung out leather arms to every room
and flogged the mill's machines to screaming work.
The mill began to thrum and rattle
and grind out food for men and cattle.

No artless system this; conveyors tall
with subtle clutches caught the flying wheel,
pinion revolved on gear, ratchet and pawl
performed efficient ministry to meal:
from flashing knives that ran and howled in pits
to where, in a last swaying shaker croft,
reached by a frail stairway hung on air,
the last slim belt brought the last corn aloft.
And at the end of this near-endless chain,
the miller's sack drew down the golden grain.

One secret of the mill's success was this:
no time was wasted on what wouldn't run.
All outworn mechanisms soon were sent
to lumber rooms until the age was done:
dim, drowsy, dreaming rooms of dusty iron,
of steelyards, pulleys, engines set aside
to wait repair, which might be slow to come;
they'd not the first call on the miller's pride.
Newer, more useful, intricate machinery
consumed his interest in his modern granary.

He thought still less of spidered cellar rooms
which held the mill's first boilers lying dead,
uncharged and fireless, stripped of what could be
some use in operations overhead:
archetypes of power, the legends of the mill,
with tales of harvests handled in a day
and prodigies of stokers. So great kings
are seen far off, but will resume their sway
in other ages. Dark now the high hall
where the spear-shadows tossed upon a wall.

OLD ELLERMAN

Old Ellerman would stump around the yard
rearranging tomatoes:
culls and rottens, half-ripes on the bottom,
fine fruit on the top rows.

Forty years of grubbing a sand farm
on the Decker Road
had taught him every lawful way there was
to stack a crooked load.

Satisfied finally with his handsome hampers
and his fine chicanery,
he'd watch the wagon roll off down the road
to Nowaskie's cannery

and watch it rolling back an hour later,
a total rejection:
Nowaskie knew enough to look beneath
a hamper's fine complexion.

Then would Old Ellerman storm, and stamp the ground,
at his foiled camouflage,
as though in a dim way earth had cheated him,
and if he couldn't pass the loss around,
why then, he had a right to rage.

MORNING

Slow, slow
this morning.

Slow as sun that rose
on Sumer and Akkad.
Dawn agricultural   human
full of silence and
the sleep of children.

The kitchen's ticking clock stopped.
Time is
light sliding down walls
quietly,
quietly
broken under the lintel,
a level light that tips
downward, dropping
the clock, the calendar
back into shadow.

Four thousand years
of morning in the swept house,
of yet-to-be-spoken
human speech   instrument
gong struck slowly against silence,
of the child to be wakened,
his sleeping face
the face of Sumer and Akkad.

AMERICAN ARCHAEOLOGY

In October,
dry fists of wild carrot,
blue-flaming chicory, puffs of boneset
on a road that led
into the woods.

Where the road broke up were fragments
of an old stone road.
By chance I had found
my great-great-grandfather's path
northward from Utica Ferry
to the new Indiana lands;
the road preserved by neglect
in this one spot.

What there is
of American archaeology
survives mostly this way.
I have come upon old graves
on hilltops, between fields,
stones sunk in hummocky ground.
Once, searching
for the lost town of Turpey,
I saw the road to it
from a half mile away,
tunnel of light through trees,
but when I reached the trees
the road was gone.

A Tory told me
something about America:
Philip Hawk, actor
in a Bicentennial tent show,
who in the guise of a cobbler taught us
to skive leather,
use a half-moon knife,
and talked quietly about how hard it is
to follow conscience.

An old road keeps itself
long after men don't,
its bench and camber
plain under the sod,
a traversable way
and deep this fall
in wildflowers:
feverfew, boneset,
the blue heal-all.

THE SHIPYARD

The shipyard lies
next to our journeys,
between highway and river,
gray field
of rising and falling sculpture.
Driving past
we consider shipfloors,
seawalls, whalecages,
here a hill of bollards rusting,
there a truck piled
with silver valves.

A crane moves in
throwing ropes.
A workman hooks them to corners
of a hatch cover.
The ropes tighten,
he jumps off just in time.

All winter the yard
is a camp of fires,
big oil-drum heaters roaring,
orating to frozen crowds.
At 3:30 the gates open,
men barge out in smoke,
laughing, blocking our cars,
banging on trunks
if we manage to bluff them out,
going home to TV.
One day they strike

and everything stops.
The yard waits.
Signs tilt back and forth,
there is coffee on card tables.
Wives come with scarves holding
hair heaped in rollers
like rows of boiler pipe.
Unfair, unfair.

The company gives in,
ships resume.
We never see them finished,
but one day they are gone.
And meanwhile
we have had a wedding day,
brought children home,
hurried to work.
From the house on the crane, someone
has watched us go by.

ON THE DIFFICULTY
OF CHANGING ANYTHING

This herringbone terrace gets shabbier
each year. I remember laying it out,
neat as a new suit, a careful weave
of old bricks on sand, but they didn't wear well.
Each winter crushes more of them in its hand.
Spring pries the fingers open and sifts
down dust and crumbs of red rock.

Gradually the terrace becomes what it is,
a barren of small weeds, miniature shrubs
in bombed squares. Ants pursue
private purposes among the ruins.
Vines creep over the inscriptions.
Sometimes for days no one passes.

A new patio would be better,
but we delay and leave the old terrace there,
like a suit we don't wear and won't throw away,
a habit we can't shake. The grass
grows up in angled rows, remembering
where the bricks were,
as permanent now as Carthage.

A CHILD'S SONG OF SPACE

Space is the out there
that is not out there,
that *is* the not out there.
It is endless but star-bounded,
rounding on itself.
Small as a pin,
wide as a window,
this is space.
When something is in it,
it is not space.
When nothing is in it,
it is not space either.
It cannot be emptied or filled.
It is the big dark
cupboard full of stars.

STILL-LIFE WITH MYSTERY

The clock ticking
above a table with
six new wine glasses,
litter of papers,
smoking coffee,
and a note:
"So, you've found me!
Well, you won't stop me!
Tomorrow I unleash
Microbe X!"

II

A PROBLEM OF ART

Once when I was a small child I painted
a watercolor landscape, green to the flat
horizon, then an azure sky—
halves of pure color. Everyone laughed
and gave it names, like "Summer Pasture
Just After the Cows Have Gone Over the Hill."
I didn't mind, knowing my work would last,
and that the critics, though dim, were not unkind.

I think that was the high point of my career
in art. Complexities multiplied
from then on. I have been trying bit by bit
to get back to that purity of line
and color, but I cannot simplify
enough. Those cows keep getting into it.

!

Sirius exclaiming
in the morning sky.

THE CONQUEST OF SPACE

If I lie and look up
through dill,
the moon's nail holds
a floret
like a cup.

If I look out
past the wet wire,
I cannot tell
bright water
from a star.

61 DEGREES NORTH

Only once I went as far north as I could
and saw the Yukon stampeding north all night
like a green freight train. Too long.
No sunsets came, and every time
I looked out, that damn river was still there.

I don't want many things to last forever,
or to live without sunsets going up
like shouts of gold. I think I know
why prospectors went dumb or crazy. Those days
were as near eternity as I want to come.

HOLY CROSS CITY

Jeep trails reach some of them still,
those grassed-over gold camps, derelict
by Victorville, but no one goes
to Holy Cross City. The road to it
washed out longer ago than anyone
remembers, and the giddy narrow gauge
never climbed there from the settlements.
It was the highest camp, and cold
as thrift, a ghost town even then
in tales for boys and scarecrow wanderers.
"If nothing pans out here, I'll head
for Holy Cross," they said, as if to say,
"Don't look for me again." It was a place
to travel light to, when your luck had gone.

PASSAGE

This passage seems to be a doubtful voyage,
driven on by lightning, on an unsteady keel,
the crew in irons, a venture that could still
end well or just as easily miscarry,
the partners in port, their minds on arbitrage,
the one unsealed instruction, not to despair.

METAPHOR

Tangles of language, the pleached roots of trees
belong to metaphor, which is itself
a metaphor for something strangely human,
the old desire to go
deeper into the forest, carrying
baskets of fire to find a signature.

Nothing requires that words or trees be more
than what they are. It is enough
to say "these words," "this tree." What goes
beyond that is cedar and silver,
given for the hammered gates of Nineveh,
for praise, and the delight of praise.

THE DREAM OF BOY BLUE

The trees lay down their shadows
like Bibles. They are perfect now
in this windless light,
and the world is perfect around them.

All the farms have been wound
and are keeping time,
keeping time.
The haymow lowers its little windlass,
the toy corn canters
into a meadow of milk and wool.
Sleep, murmurs the hay,
sleep.

This is the dream of Boy Blue.
This is the door behind the clock
that led to the house that Jack built.
This is the room
of pewter and blue delft.
See how the firelight shone on all of it!—
on the polished oak of the settle,
the cask of apples, and the little
golden horn on the shelf.

Open any door, she told him,
except one.

Opening it, he found himself
on a road cast over the landscape
carelessly, like a ribbon on a breast.
A gold note hung in the trees,
the signal to set out.

HARDTACK'S VERANDAH
(For my father)

Hardtack's verandah! All the carpenters
in town got drunk one summer building it
and chivvying Hardtack and each other on
to grander schemes, until finally it had
enough gingerbread to sink a steamboat,
with twenty-nine columns and a gilded promontory
on which a brass band could have played at ease.
When it was done, the men stood up to pose
with Hardtack and his house, and someone made
a poem to celebrate the folly and record
how many trees had lain down for the saw
so that at any hour Hardtack could have shade.

And trees are beautiful, but not as beautiful
as a verandah, or a chair or cupboard
brought to use
by human artifice,
or are not beautiful in the same way.
You knew that
with your carpenter's grasp of things.

"My father is a poet, he makes things,"
the speaker in a novel said, and it was true,
or seemed so, yet not every carpenter
who cobbles up a porch has fathered art
from the ruck of unsawn wood or words,
or has the look that Hardtack's workmen had:
sly and surprised, triumphant, a little mad.

Say it another way. I think it must be
like fishing off the long pier at St. Joe
on a foggy morning when the pier's the only
thing in sight, and there may be nothing clear
to Michigan (the poet baits his hook
with words and for them), and a bass strikes
and climbs on shining scales out of the dark.

I wrote this at the desk you made for me
with secret drawers. I found them all except
the one holding the secret of all art.

WHAT THE DEAD ARE TRYING TO TELL US

Tonight the long sun leans
across a little valley, sets fires
in what seem windows
on the other hillside,
but are not windows, are graves,
each polished stone a tongue of flame.

Is it a semaphore the dead are using
to tell us something, or only
some unexhausted energy, the phosphor
of corpse candles?
Neither, of course.
The light flies back
no differently than from the moon,
that great flying grave
as poxed and unreadable
as an old tombstone.
The dead do not communicate that way.

I read it in a letter
mislaid for years: "Your grandfather
once told me when he was very old,
'I hope to die
with the taste of strawberries in my mouth.'"

THE MOVEMENT

I saw them from the highway
for a moment: brown cattle moving
out of a field the sun was grazing
into a woods. They seemed to be
moving together though not in unison,
their separate motions knitted,
purposive, slow.
It was a different rhythm,
and pleasing somehow that they moved
between light and dark, although the direction
seemed not to matter (it could have been
dark into light, and these
any animals night-drowsed in a field),
but the movement—
there was something about that.

VANDERHOOF'S ETCHING

He knew
just how the rails fell out
of an abandoned fence
two fields from the house,
and how a birch
took root unnoticed
on the pasture side.
Beyond, some birds
flew on toward winter night.
It is undated,
being for all times true.

My uncle kept it
almost 50 years.
It made him think
"of fence corners of youth,"
he said, and on the back
told how he wrote
to Mrs. Vanderhoof and got
asked out to tea
by two brave, aged sisters
in New Jersey
(the sketch an unanticipated gift).

Now it is mine,
or so much mine
as truth or any work of art
can be. I'm glad it has
no people, or that they
are here vicariously
in fence and house. Snow lies
unsmooth in the weeds, and more
is coming soon.
There is an absentness
that soothes.

Dave Carlson says
of some grave, one-day crisis,
"I suppose
this hasn't caused a ripple on the rings
of Saturn."
I'll stay closer home and add,
"Nor has it blown
one dry leaf off that birch
or caused
a single bird to falter
in that sky."

THE WATER WITCH

Witching for water is like having
a stitch in the side. The first time,
when I was 12, it was a catch
that made the apple branch
twist in my hands. They dug
and found water 70 feet down.
After that, they took me everywhere.
I got to know
that country down to bedrock,
where every spring was, where
to dig cisterns or make
a reservoir for cattle.
Luck, some called it,
others said a gift.

I've laid awake and wondered
why any man should be so daft
on water. I've seen it
in dreams, like silver strings
lacing the dark, or nerves.
Sometimes I've dreamed it
in cloudy rooms
with fish around my feet.
My brothers all had farms

and did well. I never worked
when I could witch for water.
Sometimes I've wondered
if it is a gift
and who the giver was,
and if I'd give that gift back
if I could.

ON THE ROUTE IN AUGUST

This Sunday on the route my son wore shoes
for the first time since May.
It was a fine day, but colder. Full of news,
I trundled up the block and stayed on guard
for dogs (one learns to lay
the papers softly). My son slipped out of view
on porches and in morning-shadowed yards
to surface suddenly
a block away. I've had routes that were harder,

starting at nine. My mother let me pass
the North End, a collector
of gray coins in a year of war and loss.
She thought to teach me life, and anyhow
"a route builds character,
and he can win a bike." This from the boss,
half-right. My character is better now
(but I don't vector
the papers quite as well, my arm is slower).

Today we saw the first leaves on the walk.
The gardener's small beer
of thrift-shop zinnias, tipsy on their stalks,
heard autumn's long note like a semibreve
announce the closing year.
I thought it must be time again to talk
with Old Man Ferguson: "Well, boy, I've paved
a few more miles and fear
that my immortal soul is not yet saved."

He said it every fall, then saved or not
dropped off the route. One thinks
of people less than house numbers and lots.
The people quit, the houses stay a while.
Even here memory shrinks.
Where did I come in on the Third Street route
those winter mornings with my wits congealed
to the muzzy smell of drink
in upstairs flats, and young wives in chenille?

But I remember carrying the *Star*
downtown and going in
Marone's to watch fat Wilfred mop the bar
around the drunks, the pickled tongue, and punchboards.
I grew up on a Schwinn
that threw me overboard one morning near
the car-parts store. I looked up from the curb
at Miss Milwaukee's grin,
her parts a shock it took a while to absorb.

There's less excitement on this present dull
suburban paper trail,
but there's still something of a voyeur's pull.
This morning early, opening a screen,
I heard someone exhale
behind an open shade. Not to unlull
that sleep, I laid a paper on the swing
and looked out at the rail.
There is an honor in this sort of thing.

35

It will be winter soon. So let it come;
a paper boy requires
only a little light. One Christmas some
first riser had been out to set a frieze
of luminary fires
that separated darkness from his home.
(So homesteads in the Outer Hebrides
raised lamps aloft like stars
and set a term to desolated seas.)

UPSTATE DAYS

It was a grand country
for painless dentistry, perpetual motion.
Any farm boy with gumption could
dig up a mastodon or walk out
of a potato field and get rich

building octagon houses
or filling dazzled heads
with words like "philoprogenitive"
and "amativeness." Enlightenment blazed
from Short Tract to Shongo.

Sometimes it seemed as if dreams
had clabbered like stars
in winter over Cohocton
and wouldn't thin out until you carried
the whole U.S. of A. in your grip

to board the Erie. All those airy
rooms and through-lights glowed
with tallow-headed farm boys reading
all night after the chores
and supper, chaste as Shakers.

Why, sometimes success
would just walk up and shake hands
with a bright young man willing
to work hard and stay up late
in the potato kingdom,
in the buckwheat capital of the world.

WITH TIME

Reading, you slept and let
the tale go on alone.
I traced your cheekbone's edge
under the graying helmet,
valor's visible badge
above invisible bone.

The light across the bed
lent a severe note
to your long-loved face
so that I meditated
how time finds each child out
of all its hiding places.

But that's not what was meant.
The tale was incomplete.
Even as it wars against
inevitable defeat,
the body leaps and sings
and capers into spring.

We will both be undone,
but not before tomorrow.
There will be time to learn
to love you out of sorrow,
to love the luminous bone
after all else has burned.

BELIEVERS

The young missionary, modest, sincere,
waited, papers in his hand, to ask
if I would help him. His First Century flock,
housed in a rented classroom at a school,
had sent him to approach me with the task
of editing its discipline. William Zinsser
and other inerrant masters of the rules
had led him only into writer's block.
I was suggested for stylistic rescue.
Who could resist such being looked up to?

Ten chapters. I began to mark the pages,
remarked the curious insularity
of fundamental belief, but as I read
began to be attracted, not by faith
but by a sort of bright simplicity.
The preacher's writing, flawed, still had a breadth
that now and then broke through the dry "thus saiths"
to fire his dogma with a loving rage.
The work grew serious. Could my close correction
bring his revealed thought into perfection?

The one true church is usage. Now with more
of grammardom's especial gauds and bangles,
I argued like an Alexandrine priest
on triune God, wrote codices explaining
commas, communed with Crabb upon the least
preciosity of adjectival meaning:
has each a unique link to oneness, or
has oneness the uniquity? O angels
on pins! Could I be starting out
to tinge his boyish certainty with doubt?

Or was it, perhaps, the other way around,
me being led on? "In Lystra there was only
a handful of believers, for *all* stood
round about Paul." Suddenly the scene grew
to frightened men, their teacher on the ground
now rising with fearful slowness from the stones,
striking his clothing, wiping away blood . . . .
It was as though a staring traveler through
an antique port had said, "It was like that.
I saw it, and I never could forget."

My secretary received and sent the sheets,
becoming just that intermediary
the preacher loathed, a priestess of the word.
I stayed aloof, lost sleep, and read St. Paul,
and saw what else enthralled my missionary:
not incident, but the terrible and sweet
society of those who can lose all
for God or grammar, mankind or the sword.
I watched a sun-spar sweep a printed stack,
draw words out of the dark and thrust them back.

The end grew near. The next and final galleys
were edited. He settled up the bill
with thanks. The finished manuscript, he said,
was perfect and would lead his flock aright.
We never met again. I see him still,
a journeyer through shabby rooms up alleys
adrift in time, his followers met to read
that flawless scripture and to pray for light,
led on by two stars on a darkening sea,
their preacher's faithful words, my zealotry.

THE STORM

The light, not thunder, woke us out of bed:
at first a silent drumming on the shutter
as though a pole were burning, then a muttered
complaint that grew to argument, then rout.
Sheet lightning fell, like quick blows overhead
by someone having his total temper out.

That huge discharge of current in the air
startled the suburb into nervous daylight.
We ran to see. Alternate black and white,
like a mad *paparazzo* going amok,
snapped your astonished photo down the staircase.
Even the kitchen chairs were thunderstruck.

Was it awe of violence that kept us
at windows until the storm moved farther off,
or a regard more primitive, the stuff
of ancient and propitiatory spells
against disorder or the stunned perception
of some high order alien to ourselves?

No news at 2 a.m. We shuffled back
to bed. I dreamed a peaceful scene at sea,
where a small boat was bringing steadfastly
a grave, gray-wimpled figure to the shore,
who became Ruth, wearing her German frock,
and kicked to splinters the apartment door.

Love breaking in? The crime's more likely mooching
around outside, or bothering the machine.
"We're sorry, at the moment we're not in.
Please leave your name and message at the beep."
(But someone's really there in the dark listening,
or making love, or maybe just asleep.)

Or else the ones who love us most don't phone
and go away, so that we won't suspect
a loitering and call the house detective.
Of all the appealing letters in the mail,
love goes back easiest "Address Unknown."
Could love be otherwise and still be real?

This morning wires are down, a neighbor bails
sewage from his basement, lawns are full of lees.
We meet to swap survivors' histories,
begin rebuilding, laugh, and leave behind
the sleeping thought of order neither frail
nor irresistable, but not unkind.

THE TREE NEXT DOOR

looks like someone stuck
into the ground headfirst
up to the waist. I want to find
the secret behind the world.

III

III

EYE

If this window were a seascape,
the red car in the middle distance
would be a ship hanging
halfway up a gray wall of water.

I pick up "eye" and carry it around.
It turns when I do, bends,
gets up and down, looks
under, over, and inside things.

It is attached to "brain,"

which can be fooled. Last night I walked
behind a man who was walking faster
down Walnut Street. He shrank
until he was the same size

as television people,
then disappeared in the end
of a green tunnel. Eye,
how shall I be well

and artfully deceived today?

THE SCHOOLROOM

Its pulldown mural taught us all we knew
of earth and sea—
ocean unscrolled its letters on a blue
profundity that shoaled into a *bay*
lapping an *isthmus*.
A *plain* rose gradually
into a *mountain*,
and much more
in this ideal landscape,
the perfect country of words.

Words were the object.
The signs edging the board,
the blue-backed speller's drifting spars,
were messages washed toward
those solitary islands where we stood
with paper and our crayons neatly turned,
yellow and *red*, to draw
the *ship* that soon would ferry us
into the future's difficult
ungraded school.

There wasn't a day we didn't wake
expecting landfall, or a night
when sudden headlands
might not block the stars.
O uncorrupted country
where the pure word
was laid across the faultless brow
of earth, and the unsullied
river ran down the *valley*
to the *sea*.

THE IDEA OF DOMINION

These immaculate farms go for miles
through not-really-blue grass. The fields
are fenced, and within them other fences
protect trees or seal arroyos where
a horse might stumble. Much care
is evident, the horses less so,
as though forgotten in the large plan
for which they were excuse. One senses,
even in lazy weather, behind
ambition's brightwork serious intent,

and behind intent the idea of dominion.
That way of thinking begins early
and continues, so that seeing
a magazine's abstract photo
of scrap metal, roofing perhaps,
crumpled like geologic strata,
the mind sees a sort of col going up
and thinks it could climb that slope
and plant its tiny flag on the highest
rolled edge of the metal world.

Dominion over everything? As children
we made each bare mound
of builder's earth into a mountain laced
with our roads and tunnels.
Our toy trucks crept in perfect order
along gorge and precipice. We held
them in life and it was
a world—an intention
that was ours only, a domain
of serious children.

Or earlier, when I crawled
under my mother's Singer, on the treadle,
the cast-iron undercarriage soared
over me, a vaulting conception
of half-dark galleries and catwalks
where the huge wheel plunged
at my will and dominion.
What does this mean? Nothing.
You can say, "Nothing. I'm tired,
and don't want to think of it."

Chincoteague Island in the Old Dominion
still has its wild and unfenced horses.
A friend told how a pony,
scenting food one afternoon, walked
through the side of her tent, slicing it
with surgical hooves, then walked
out the other side, an act
of perfect freedom. The tent
was torn irreparably, she said,
"yet for some reason we were happy."

PHRASE FROM A LETTER

My father has forgotten the word "magnolia."
"What are those trees with the pink blossoms,"
he asks, "that bring on ice storms?"
I can remember that but have lost
so much else that was precious—
friend's faces, the smell of wisteria
heaped over the springhouse, the color
of lilacs broken and gathered
years ago in an alley. We joke
about Sherlock Holmes and the finite capacity
of the brain, but it's true, it's true.

And now you are leaving the country
you told me of—the dikes and orchards
we saw together. Already the future
holds out its foxfire promises to us.
The past's precise apples darken and fall.
"I have forgotten so much of my life here."

THE DARK

The way we fill houses with light—
it wasn't always so. In Babylon
night had its own deep kingdoms
and farms. Think of a town of mud houses,
or stone, going to sleep
with no candles or fire, no light
at the corner, nothing after dark.
People would be there, but as withdrawn
in their stone city as the dead in theirs.

Or imagine a northern forest with day fading
to a last white tarnish on the river
before dark. After that nothing
until morning. Later, in villages,
watchmen called curfew—cover the fire—
and people went lightless to bed
with cows and chickens. Rousing anyone
was like breaking a spell or turning
rusted locks in centuries of sleep.

Does it matter that we are losing stars
in light? And what of dreams?
We don't know if they've changed.
One night I argued eloquently
for a woman's life. It was no one I knew
and more real than anything that has happened
before or since. In darkness the earth turns
outward upon the wide gaze of space.
Night holds us for a time in its velvet mouth.

MY WIFE DANCES WITH OUR SONS

Where did they come from,
these tall men who laugh
and are light on their feet?
We didn't mean . . . we never . . .
we just . . . . Oh, no,
that wasn't it at all.

QUARRELING THROUGH THE LOUVRE

We fought
from one end of history
to the other. It started
by Hammurabi's iron law
and raged
upstairs and down
through centuries
of terra cotta,
bronze, and travertine.
Nobody heard a thing.
By the Winged Victory
of Samothrace we lost
our heads completely.
You traipsed off to rest
your aching feet
among the Fragonards.
I went to sulk beside
the untranslatable Etruscans
and the perfect Venus
whose foot is broken.

Now we're flying west
on separate planes.
You don't remember
what we quarreled about,
or won't say.
Why is it always
my story that gets told,
and yours that's put away
with the rolled-up cycloramas
in the cellar?
Where's the stone
to solve this silence,
these clay tablets
with letters like thorns?

ASH LIMBS

There's a connection
between the way the ash tree's broken limbs
lie in the driveway and the way we lie
    in bed afternoons.

So much left undone
that we ought to have done, but now it seems
right to let yard and garden be themselves
    a while without shame,

    and to be ourselves.
Already, gray-green lichens fur the limbs,
a complex landscape whose blown spore cases
    resemble craters.

The bark has fallen
away from one limb, showing the heart chased
intricately. So many lives go on
    we hardly know them,

    as I hardly know
your long-haired portrait now that your hair lies
coarse and abrupt as a fan of lava
    stopping a fair field.

We will rise in time,
good citizens, to clear the ash-strewn drive
and add the rubbish to a backyard heap
    that shelters juncos.

There it will soften
to mulch or (if we don't keep lookout) be
burnt by our crazy neighbor who likes fire.
   The ash will ascend

      in its beautiful
changes, as you are beautiful and changed,
as we are changed, maybe to nothing less
   than our human selves.

WHAT WE DID IN JULY

One night we sat on the porch arguing
about whether that light coming in
was a plane or a star.
Oh, and we threw the papers out
without reading them.
Yesterday Karen walked to the end
of the block and found
another block beyond that.
Maybe someday . . . .
I spent a week looking at the penholder
with the Chinese characters
for "Be Patient."
One day the cat and I hoed the garden.

THE BIRDS & ME

I didn't have a poem,
a song, for you,
something your own,
who claim to be
so resolutely unpoetic—
nothing to give you,
no more than the birds have,
who take your suet
and thistle, filling
the backyard with their
undedicated songs.

GOING UNDER THE HOUSE

The door is hidden
in the bedroom closet
under a rug. Two boards lift up.
Sit on the edge a moment
and check your gear—a flashlight,
goggles, maybe a hammer.
Wear a long-sleeved set
of your oldest sweats, ones your wife
can throw out afterward.
Now parachute in,
and when you hit the dirt, roll
into this country's basic posture,
supine. Notice the low sky
of poplar, the scattered points
of flooring nails, and over there
a sheet of cardboard
someone left who thought
he could keep clean. In the distance
a few stars will be shining
through the fundament.

Time to move out.
Travel is painfully
slow here. Your back will feel
each rock and spall of brick.
Try not to mind it. Use the joists
to pull yourself forward
(backward, I mean)
past the cold-air return. Now turn
what would be right

if you could stand upright
and look ahead.
When you are parallel
to the joists and have headroom,
scrunch your way toward
the foundation vent's
distant, dusty sun.
(The door you came in by will have become
a dim moon over your left shoe.)

Soon, on your right, you'll pass
a central massif of brick—chimney rock,
the natives probably call it.
Keep going. Take off
your goggles, which will have fogged
in the heat. Don't stop long.
It's always hard
to start again.

When you reach the farthest corner,
lie quietly in a comfortable
hollow of dirt. Let your eyes close,
your neck muscles relax.
Listen. Can you hear
anyone moving upstairs,
the low mumble of TV, a car
infinitely far off?
Try not to sleep. That's
fatally easy. Try to remember
your reason for coming here.

CATCHES

The poem in the dream was clear
about stanzaic form, but it would not
go into language, even though I ran
uphill behind it, coaxing. It was
a lovely brindled poem, but it ducked
each time I swung my poem net.

After a while I sat down in the dream
to catch my breath and watch
the morning show. Some trees put down their feet
through fog, like elephants. I thought
this was unusual, to see these trees
with dripping pads and toes. What next?

Next, I woke up and couldn't remember much
about the poem or trees, except
that trees were easier to catch than poems.
So I got up and went outside and looked
at trees, and each one had a foot and toes,
just as the dream had said it would.

WITNESS

In the corner window of an old building,
a pot of flowers, common
geraniums in a cream jar,
seen daily against
different backgrounds—
sometimes a lighted room
or black rectangle
of reflected sun
or at night a shadow,
but always
the detail organizing the landscape.

Sometimes the flowers
became a face looking out
of a retired life, an invalid
watching years turn
in the turning of leaves, in shapes
of snow on cornices.
Under the window in spring
were found bits of paper
with here and there a word.

He was inventing the world. Each day
resolved itself in his gaze
as a painting starts
from the eye of the helmeted
man in the foreground, his hand raised
toward a prospect of smoke and horses,
his mouth beginning to form
a word: "Behold!"

TO A WRITER
WHO HASN'T WRITTEN YET

"I don't know how,"
you said. Who does?
I want to hear your voice,
not what you say,
but something else, the note
that's yours—a bird
starting up now outside
in darkness, its throat
rusty with sleep,
hauling the sun up
on a bent pin of song.

THE SOLDIERS
(Pfc. Stephen Bridges, Co. E, 152nd Infantry)

So we drove down into the delta
that summer, the land leveling
to red fields with here and there a cabin
stooped in the Mississippi heat, and reached
Hattiesburg and Camp Shelby—eight-man tents
along roads bordered with white stones.
This was the first year of the war.

My artist uncle was going to that war.
My father and grandfather took turns
driving the Ford. I lay in the back
on brown plush, pushing my finger through
a cigarette burn. Old men in overalls
pumped Blue Crown into reservoirs marked off
in gallons. Already the young men were gone.

Why was an artist going to a war?
I didn't know. This journey was a lark.
I sat with my greasy sack of fried potatoes
from the roadside diner and looked out
at miles of cotton, wider than Indiana.
What did I know of artists or their wars?
His letter written that year would have meant nothing,

and even later had to be pieced out,
the way he helped illiterate troops write home,
from partial knowledge: "Medieval thought
cannot be simply grasped," he wrote, and then
"We go to the range tomorrow"—two perspectives
from this ex-Benedictine who would go
to the South Pacific and nearly die,

but live to leave his artist's testimony
on the bright, anonymous glass walls
of aisles and apses. "I am incapable
of your detachment. Any age that seeks
truth is of value. The medieval mind
interests me only for its real values
beyond all fabulous gullibility."

Buna had fallen. I put the Solomon Sea
into my scrapbook. My uncle never talked
of war, except once when he said he went
"rather than miss my generation's history"
or spoke respectfully of those recruits
who signed their names with Xs on his letters.
Later we found his medals in a box.

February 16, 1942.
How easily the thought of the letter moves
from matters of divisional supply (his job)
to the four historical divisions
of Vincent de Beauvais, four ages of truth.
"A truth never checkmates another truth,
for if it did the whole structure would fall.

"Let no affirmation be suppressed,
until a new Aquinas comes to gather
them all into one sheaf, to the least fragment."
All this was hidden from a boy of seven
in Mississippi, asleep on the back seat
of a hot Ford, or drinking Royal Crown
in country stores along the Pascagoula,

as it is hidden still, in part. I know
that looking for truth is sweating, swearing work,
an island war, as difficult as getting
butter from a duck, a delta farmer said,
or in my uncle's sober second thought,
nearly a lifetime afterward, "Sometimes
it's all you can do to think one simple thing."

His thought was love. The artist gathered glass
into the images of saints and fused
irreconcilables of lead and light.
Around him as he worked, the soldiers stood.

AND SUDDENLY FLOWERS

Coming down fast off the interstate,
I brake on the ramp, and suddenly flowers
are everywhere, blue and white:
chicory, Queen Anne's Lace
flood over the pavement.
The car rocks a moment,
steams, falls quietly apart.
I want to jump up, shout,
start running into the flowers
that stretch farther into the future
than I can imagine.

ONE OF THE DEATHS

This is one of the deaths that we can die,
the one of daily life, so useful
(so good) that we never see
how it is all luminous—
the impeccable chastity of the snow,
how winter light slices
the tunnel at the end of the street,
how the vole's eye shuts
under the root of the mulberry,
or how a star may hang
for a million years in the same place.

WHAT REALLY WAS

What really happened?
We remembered the past
as definite, or thought we did.
We remembered something,
but the light was all wrong.

Those houses, whose were they?
And that clear morning, timed
to the tick of now?
These photos, crisp
as paper embers,
and the people
whose laughter was real,
not recollected,
your face in the train,
Margaret's kiss—all dear
as clutched coins,
and irretrievable?

What really was withdraws
along night roads and leaves
these propped vedettes.
Whatever happened then
was fresh as paint. It just
walked out one morning
without saying goodbye.

THE MANSIONS ON SOUTH THIRD

In April light, these deft
and dazzled leaves have left
no stone safe on its stone.

Blurred by a scrim of trees,
the scrolled securities
of porch and roof go down

below the riffling wind.
One who had been my friend
is gone,

and through no more than leaf
marble is told of grief
and granite overthrown.

NARRATIVE

Waking in a room you don't know
for a moment
where you are. Someone
has gathered it around you
as you slept—
wheeled in the bureau,
painted the woodwork green,
hung Monet's fake snapshot.
You wake into a narrative
that seems familiar
but is really no place like home.

"Isn't narrative just a snapshot?"
you asked. Well, yes, maybe.
It doesn't go anywhere,
just hangs around waiting
for you to wake up. Hmmmm.
Isn't this like the old room
at home? Don't worry.
But it isn't quite,
in fact it's utterly strange
(which, if you knew it,
might frighten you to death).

Take the Monet, that old story.
Where the path begins
are two white figures.
You didn't notice the others
on the bank before,
so much like shadows,
or the boatsmoke
becoming part of a cloud,
or the letter B
whose mysterious story
is just beginning to unfold.

FOR SALLY IN HAWAII

They say that another island is coming up,
and at the other end the reefs
are wearing away. Maybe it's true.
It won't happen today. Plenty of time
to take the dogs for a walk,
glaze a pot, read something.
At night you can see the line
where the mountain turns into stars.

About that island,
it's all right not to shout
and warn everybody.
When it happens, they'll know.

IV

VI

THE ARAFURA SEA

I.

Winter in Indianapolis, and the cold
could stop your breath. Upstairs
in Ioor's stamp shop the afternoon
fell across tropic squares. Outside
the snow began, the market stank
of fish and blood, a Chinaman sold chunks
of ginger, shoveled up the twigs
of *lapsang souchong*, that tarry tea.

Revolving doors swept us
in from the snow to Ayres
at Christmas. In the bookshop we spun
the world by Cram. The shelves
of polished ebony were trig
as captain's cabins on the Indies line.
A signal scheme of muted bells
remained as ground notes in the memory.

"You have a double crown; you'll travel,"
they told me. In Berlin, Frau Grötsch
pointed to postcards of the Kaufhaus Wertheim
before the war. Her sisters carried her
to see the Christmas lights, then ran
through snow to catch the tram under a clock.
She closed the book. *Das war die schönste Zeit,
aber der Krieg hat alles weggerissen.*

II.

In the Odyssey Map Shop, a clerk unfurled
the oceans of the Indies, warm tides
that lave an archipelago—the Java Sea,
then Celebes, Molucca, Halmahera
(cupped like water in the hands); below,
the glittering chain of Bali, Flores, Savu,
Timor and Banda, and the Ceram Sea,
offering passage to the Arafura.

All night that starry sea, the Arafura,
easternmost of the eleven seas,
turned on its shelf, an ocean
of uncharted shoals, once arid, now
cloudy with brine of generation.
"Dangerous to sail," the logbook said,
"but the clear waters of the Aru Isles
afford a small and constant flow of pearls."

Coming in over the mountains, I saw
the islands spill across an evening
vibrant with bells. A lighter chuntered
in a harbor of lateen sails.
The angelus: processions of priests moved
toward the water. Just in time I saw
this was a calenture, that easy field
which tempts a sailor down to death.

III.

*After the war, we found that we had nothing
to return to. We had to make something
of where we were.* Where I am now
is here, this wintry morning,
with nothing standing but the stalks
of unnostalgic flowers, and of course
the Arafura Sea is here, the practical,
the dangerous and daily sea.

*We had a joke then: what's the difference
between a violin and a viola?
The viola burns longer.* And in truth
it takes a heap of burning
to make a house a home. Must you remember
everything? Ah, memory's a slut,
a spotted whore who'll tell
you anything you want, for free.

The other one came by in several guises.
I think I liked the maiden best,
in a gray cloak, carrying a jar
of hot soup, or perhaps the woman
at the dance, a little older, beckoning.
These are not sexual games,
although they are most deeply sexual,
and wound into the brine sea of a birth.

IV.

This was a strange country,
hard and bitter to survive in. We came
unprepared for such winters, and our homes
too far behind to help. We learned
its ways a little, but still many died.
Their graves are back there, in the land we crossed.
Mine's out ahead. I've got to go
and find it. You've your own to find. Goodbye.

Are we all aboard? The Arafura Sea
is calm tonight, and treacherously hides
its shoals. A light breeze puffs
the sails. This is no journey to a land
of longing, no warm archipelago.
The rigging slaps and groans. The lights wink out
along the coast. The native guides
look competent or murderous by turns.

The city is destroyed where I was born,
no way now but forward. All the letters
came back unanswered. No homecoming then,
only a right of passage. Driving back
in traffic, in the snow, I thought I saw
you walking toward me, your eyes
still grave and kindly. "Would you like to dance?"
you said again. Oh, yes. I would. I do.

THE SENEGALESE PHOTOS IN MONTREAL

They are arranged, certainly, to make a point,
these images of the white masters borne
or pulled in various ways by natives—
blacks usually but sometimes, oddly, Chinese—
in sedan chairs, rickshas, or on the human back.
This is Dakar, perhaps in 1904
during M. Coppolani's administration
before his murder the ensuing season
"by a band of fanatics at an oasis."
The room's other half contains the faces
of the same natives, blown up grainily
and displayed each one in its own frame.

The point is made, but still one misses the face
of the young girl posed in the ricksha,
wearing a topi with a linen band,
tiny behind her team of giant *porteurs*,
who seem content, or maybe only confused
by this strange, nearly weightless burden.
Her unusable legs are tucked beneath her
on the ricksha seat, and she grins
with the feverishness of a sick child,
the spoiled autocrat of the bedchamber,
who has been given a marvelous toy because
(but she doesn't know it) her life is ending.

AT THE HOUSE
OF NIYAMÓYOANA YABAI

Your house is empty now
in the aboriginal village,
no grain in your millet bin.
On this hot morning, light
filters through thatch
of a vacant room.
Only a tourist's foot
makes a little sound.
Your kinsmen, the little Tsou,
whose name was like the click
of birdsong or the breath note
of a wooden flute,
have almost vanished—
dead, or transformed
to dishwashers in the capital.
If I were quiet enough
would the wind say your name?
Niyamóyoana Yabai . . . .
May your name live,
may you live always
in the indestructible house
of the name.

THE WORLD AS IT IS

A friend is upset
by a statue of Kwanyin,
goddess of mercy,
in a public park.

Sure, sure, but still
there's not enough mercy
in the world as it is.

FROM A CHEAP HOTEL
AT THE EDGE OF THE KNOWN WORLD

At daybreak the rain began,
a fine veil of illusion
diffusing light
like a *shoji* screen.
I stayed in
and let sleep rinse out
its dirty laundry. Waking,
I thought of you,
how we are separated
by oceans and timezones, etc.
I was not wishing you
into this queer place, but wished
you well nonetheless.

There is not much here:
a cupboard, a cot,
something to write on.
People are friendly
but distant. Sometimes
I go a whole day
without one thought.
Over the Pacific I opened
a window and threw out
my life. It drifted down,
surprising Fred & Amelia,

who had forgotten all that.
Now I am lighter and live
on a little rice and soup.
Today a woman mistook me
for a missionary
and followed me
all over town,
asking forgiveness.

THE AIKIDO MASTER

You must know
every oiled hinge of the body,
each pivot and spring,

and how the great arc
of the world diminishes
to a locus of pain.

The task is always
to bend momentum
to your advantage,

wheeling the implacable,
onrushing force
from its orbit into yours,

until, tamed and helpless,
it follows you like a dog
trained to the leash,

and then to release it
joyfully, without rancor,
and wait.

It will come again,
unwearied, keen to exploit
your inattention.

Now it will have a knife,
now a stick. For each
you must have answers

but no final answer,
not even as, kneeling, you mime
the killing blow,

for if your secret wish
is for triumph,
you have already lost.

Most certainly,
from the beginning,
you will have lost.

BRONZE

"China's legacy of ancient greatness is her bronze ritual vessels." — Guide to National Palace Museum, Taipei

Listen, I want to tell you
about bronze: how it is mostly copper
with a little tin and lead,
how it begins in fire and smoke
of the foundry,
but its green cloak
wears out the centuries
under the earth.

You should know
how a flare-topped wine vessel, the *tsun*,
lies a millennium in the tomb
of a Shang emperor, guarded by slaves
beheaded on the runways,
and how *t'ao t'ieh*, the beast of gluttony,
grins from each of its four faces.

And know also
how the *Mao Kung Ting*, prince
of pots, bears on its inner wall
the 497 characters of royal instruction
for its founding, written
"in a stately and powerful tone"
(all this without ignoring the *chüeh*
teetering on its high legs
like a delicate drunk, or how
the *hu*'s haunches resemble
the generous buttocks of women).

Then remember
that all these pans, pitchers, buckets,
caldrons, kettles, ewers, and tubs,
with borders of cloud and lightning
and with upright handles pierced
for the thrust of carrying rods,
have come across centuries—
harried by armies, poled over rivers
at dusk, hidden in pigsties
and under the beds of peasants—
to reach the pure pause of your vision.

Imagine the bronze filled with flowers,
how water would shine
and vanish in its green gaze.

TAIPEI MOTORSCOOTER LOVE POEM

"We Reach For The Sky,
Neither Does Civilization."
What's *that*
supposed to mean,
I wonder,
and who writes
these "Chinglish" mottoes
for the sides of motorscooters?
(But I can relate
to that puckered-up pig
saying "No Kiss"
on the mudflap.)

"Heroism" is okay,
and "Dynamic Tact,"
but I prefer
"Hold Me, Enjoy
The Lovely Satisfaction
On The Road,"
which is a
"Human-Fitting
Concept," and I wish
you were here, darling,
but for now that's just
a "Nice Scene," a
"Dream 100
All I Have
Giving You
The Best Function."

LITTLE CHINESE POEM

April evening,
rustle of shore weeds
in rain-scented air,
seeds asking,
"What will my life be?"

BASHO & LANDSCAPE

A line softens into mist.
Smoke at the end of the day.
Warm rain. A few poems.

The horse will take you as far
as he knows the way, then
you must send him back

and go on alone. Beyond the barrier
is only landscape and whatever
you bring wrapped in your own skin . . . .

Oranienburg. The camps
never had trees, or any landscape
softening into dusk,

only raked fields of fire.
After a while, prisoners
ran into the wire, rather

than face an unbending gaze . . . .

Basho described islands
beyond islands, on the backs

of islands, a shining world
he dedicated to Kannon,
goddess of mercy,

who is absent in the harsh light
of superhighways, of fields
plowed under for shopping,

of thousand-year pines cut down
and hauled away by toy engines
to feed furnaces of greed,

until the world is leveled
and the islands filled in
and no sanctuary left. The origin
of landscape is mercy.

GODS, MEN, AND TIGERS

In these oracle bones,
a sense of joy at asking
and being answered:
shall the king ride out,
Father Ti, to hunt
the gold-eyed tiger?
Will Father Yi heal
the king's tooth? Such concord
of earth and heaven!

It is said
that at the wedding
of Prince Aurangzeeb,
songs and merriment
engulfed time and space.

Just now,
although I didn't ask,
sun floods this room
with morning splendor,
touching chair and table,
a philodendron, even
the sleeping cat
with holy fire.

IN THE TIME
OF THE YELLOW EMPEROR

Light comes
the way an ink drop
spreads through water,
soft conqueror.

The sky,
a pink and blue
pastel seacoast,
whitens quickly.

Days begin,
each writing
the slow calligraphy
of seasons.

Trees pass
into their yellow age,
the first winter stars
last night.

The Yellow Emperor
is said to be
still living somewhere
in the Third Court.

In the fields, smoke
of burning stubble
stings the nose. Rumors
of war persist.

RETURNING TO TAIPEI

Riding the bus down Chunghsiao
one morning, I passed
my old doorway, darkened by rain.
The courtyard tree trembled,
not in memory which cheats
because we cannot find
our place in time, but really there,
although I could not stop
or touch one leaf of it.

We also met, dear friends,
and ate together. I had forgotten
how kind your voices were,
how welcoming. Our days
came back a little as we talked,
but at a distance now,
untouchable. Too soon,
the wheel spun lazily,
bringing the fish, the fruit.
Something had happened once,
but what it was
escaped me like the rack
of morning dreams, or mist
on Yangmingshan.

You walked away and lost yourselves
in darkening air and traffic. I saw
what it had really been was love.

THE PHOTOGRAPHS OF MARTIN CHAMBI

I am lying in bed, in the dark,
thinking of the light
of Martin Chambi, who photographed
all Cuzco in the '20s and '30s,
leaving behind in the Casa Cabrera
the silver and cyan images
of Senorita Torero and the 1926
Cuzco football team,
of sloe-eyed Estelle Iberico,
belle of 1935, my birth year,
and the Fabrica de Tejidos
de Benjamin de la Torres,
motorcar emporium with statues
of Hermes and Vulcan over the door.

And I am thinking, in bed, in the dark,
of Chambi's light in the Hospital
de la Almudena as it rains down
on an invalid in her chair
through the vines of an arbor,
the name for which I have forgotten;
and also, just before sleep
overwhelms me, of the fat man
with moustaches in the photo
of the Cuzco Equestrian Club,
whose imperishable top hat
lies on the hedge before him
now and forever, as I lie in bed
in the dark, thinking of the light.

WINE TREE

At first,
only something
flickering at eyecorner,
the molle tree. (José says "moll-yuh,"
as the double L makes "yama.")
Andean willow, "tree of many vertues
casting forth small boughs
whereof the Indians make wine."
Of many names also:
Peruvian pepper,
mastick,
lentisk,
Schinus molle,
featherhead
among the serious trees.

The Incas, those Romans,
planted it beside their roads,
a green relief from sun
and all that stone.
José spots it
from the train,
leaps off,
brings back a branch
leaking its white liquor.
Tonight the whole room reeks of it.

HELLABRUN

To call it a zoölogical garden
is to be old-fashioned but accurate,
its great uncaged vistas extending
beside trees and streams, *tierpark*
with loges, with pleasances
for lions in leaves, and the name itself,
"clear spring" or "fountain," brightening
around the word "hella" like the sun
through rain, a gold shower,
and the animals in their Eden, the eland,
the giraffe and its shy cousin the okapi
beside the ibis, whose name is almost a flower.

THE TIN SINGERS

A mile out
under the Atlantic
they groped for tin.
The air rotted. They stuck
candles on felt hats,
could hear storms
roll boulders overhead.

Finishing, they rode
the beam engine's
rocking stair to grass,
a seam of singing men
who made the shaft
one mighty tremolo.
"Lord of the World-Bright Tin,"
they sang, and "Strong to Save."

The years broke them
like pit ponies,
but not their song.
I hear it on Levant's
ruined shore
this morning,
over the wasted shafts.

THE TINSMITH WHO BECAME A MIME

He could make anything
without a pattern—boxes
of all sorts, air returns,
ducts with sly junctions,
subtle cones and lames.

He grew tin-gray
with graphite, but his thought
became articulate,
and when it spoke his knives
and crimping wheels obeyed,

till in the end his shop
filled up with shapes
that no one wanted. Then
he locked the door and joined
a traveling show. For this

he shaved his head and
hung a morning coat
around his skinny bones.
Himself he sprayed tin-bright
from toe to crown.

He stands now on the margins
of the crowd, to whom
his mute and silvered presence
seems to say, "I am
the pattern for something. What?"

AN IRISH SALTSPOON
(For J, in nine-syllable lines)

The artist resisted a shamrock
(for this we should be deeply grateful),
sculpting a plain trefoil at the end
gripped easily by finger and thumb.
The bowl, tiny as a pinch of salt,
is chased with a fantastic heron,
while the back displays a Gaelic harp.
But real artistry is in the stem
where double loops like a reversed "S"
or a Victorian courtship chair
serve no purpose at all but to hold
the happy surplus of the smith's joy.

V

V

ARTIFACTS

This is the hour of the yard's
deep space, when objects
come into their own:
the blue ball abandoned
next to the fence,
chairs in a semicircle
taking tea, a toy firetruck
dripping with darkness.

And there are other things here,
some evident
as last night's bread
in its cellophane, some faint
as radio signals
from the Cenozoic—
postcards in French
from Siberia, some lines

scratched on bark:
"Leg broken, send help."
Whispers from Voyager
this morning. Jamestown
has been discovered
but it wasn't lost,
except for a little while,
except to us.

WHAT WAS PASSING

The galled catalpa's huge
misshapen bole
met me again at the end
of a night's walking.
Ivy shadowed its face
like a hand lifted
to hide a scar.
Maple and mulberry sprouted
in the rich rot of its heart.

Other objects
moved off gradually—
arbors and lawns, the stalks
of flowers bent by the wind,
houses that spoke
of neglect or care,
cars carrying
crumpled histories
into the next block.

I could see
that even the new tree
in its circle
of bricks and earth,
its fine lace glistening
with rain, was turning away,
but with such generous
and tender transience
I could let it go.

SNOWMELT

A warm day leaves only
dirty peninsulas
that rot bottom up.

Detail revives. A leaf
skitters on brown grass,
sticks sail in gutters,

floodwater hangs and flashes
over the Conrail tracks.

No more white wideness,
just the beautiful
specificity of the world.

TWO STORIES

We're sunset junkies,
but this one goes
almost unnoticed,
a slow fade
above strip malls,
barred with clouds
like an owl's feather.

It's a character
in someone else's story:
a dusk pilot, or a man
so lonesome he turns
back into the pines
and keeps going.

Here, lights come on
up and down the road
to Wal-Mart. Suns go nova
over parking lots.

In that other story,
the loss of light
is serious.
When it goes, it goes
for a long time
and over thousands of miles.

SCHOLAR AND SEAGULL

A young scholar is speaking. Behind her
a gull has flown in from Elliott Bay
and is weaving its complex aerial thread
in and out of the stone towers, "a single
event within multiple systems of meaning."

Her mind is green glass in a white lattice
across which the gull rides free in the updraft.
How long it has taken her to frame
this discourse, set forth as gracefully now
as the gull's notation on the long staff of the wind.

So much given up for this, so much gained
under the late light at the kitchen table—
years spent mastering those vast systems
in which she moves easily now, as the gull
picks effortlessly which current to seize

and to soar on, free and determined
as thought. The speaker finishes, gains
a spatter of praise. The gull climbs to its perch
in a spate of feathers. Sun breaks a little,
wanlight of winter washing the dark towers

WALKING WITH FRIENDS
THROUGH OLD-GROWTH FOREST

Deliberate slowing of the mind
among old trees—
tulip, white oak, and beech,
understory of pawpaw,
dogwood, hornbeam—
beneath which the forest floor
quickens with fern and mayapple,
with wild ginger whose blooms
are fertilized by snails, Lilo says,
it's that slow!

And Lilo and Vicco just back
from beech forests of Germany,
Mecklenburg, the lost estate—
but not bitter, just happy someone
bought and rebuilt. They tell us
how Germany is turning back
and tearing out quick fixes
of the post-war. Vicco's news,
of all those wartime cities
blazing with color now,

offers hope. Though nothing stays
there is some reason to build, restore.
The mind has to slow down to see
that this forest was never virgin,
was always touched by everything
except man—a complex candle
burning down, rising to heaven,
in which all impulses to save, destroy
are reconciled and we walk,
dazzled by light,
where the canopy broke and fell.

THE LANDSCAPE DEEPER IN

These woods at summer's end
resist the eye's onslaught—
the walnut's cantering leaves,
the maple's lowered lance,
the oak's close-fisted hold,
setting the gaze at naught.
Under them, all is greaved
in weeds. Not till they go
will something let us see
the landscape deeper in—
will something lead the eye
past elemental limb
to find the mounded burrow,
the rock within the shade,
the lightning-scrivened tree—
will something raise a cry
across the field's last furrow,
striking the shield aside,
and give us leave to see.

WRITING A POEM

It's like making fire by friction.
Begin with nothing, then find
a stick with the right curve, limber
enough to string with rawhide.
Next take a punky board and cut
a V notch (look for a spindle
of the same stuff). Use something harder
for the handhold that cups
the turning spindle. Finally
slip into a graveyard after dark
and steal bark from a cypress tree.
Now you're ready. Bow the spindle,
balancing weight and speed,
until a spark glows in the notch.
Knock it into the bark and blow.
Fire will come to you out of nothing
but your own desperate need.

LETTER TO PORT TOWNSEND
(For Mike and Ling-hui O'Connor)

Dear Mike, When I was a kid, solving
the map puzzle, it was always good—
after square Wyoming and kinky Idaho—
to reach Washington and find
wheat fields and orchards, and the corner
where the ocean had bitten into the state
like a ripe apple.

So it was good to visit you
and Ling-hui in your old town
that might have been Seattle
but wasn't, where there is just
the madrone tree on its precipice
and the Sound falling away
toward Mount Baker and the Three Fingers.

It is early here, and a kind
of Indiana typhoon rattles the window
where I write, but the mental weather
is still Port Townsend. I am half persuaded
to go with you again
on a margin of driftwood, kelp, and stones
to the Port Townsend Light

and the old gun turrets
that guard against no enemy now
but the sea. I think we would not say
anything much this time, only look.
I read your West Irish book
on the plane. Great Blasket and "the vanishing"
broke my heart, but what can one do?

At the other end of the map were rocks.
Gradually, each headland was lit
and then the spaces between,
until Newfoundland from Cape Race
to Corner Brook and the Norse Light
rose blazing like a candelabrum
out of the Atlantic.

There is only this world to live in—
obdurate, strange—and only what work
one can do, from whatever place
is temporarily habitable. The job
is marginal, and each abandoned place
another in a line of fires
marking the edge of the sea.

The wine with your poem on the label
flew safely, but may not age longer
than this Thanksgiving. Tell Hui
that a recipe is coming
for the Dutch rolls. With those
and two salmon she can feed
5,000 poets. Love to you both, Bill.

MESSAGES

In today's mail,
photos of women
burned in Jakarta

and a letter
asking me to sign
a card because

some prisoners hear
no human voice
but their torturer's.

Tonight someone
has chalked
"I love you"

on the sidewalk
by the supermarket,
and again,

a little further
into the dark,
"I love you."

THE NEW YORK GIRL
(A typewriter poem)

A house. A family. Henry. Myrtle. Me. A building
like a grand palazzo with fantastic balustrades.
People come and go and one of them (transparent)
is the New York Girl, who comes to visit, stays,
is around---a friendly sort, our sort-of friend.
Henry and she trade looks, poems, chili recipes.
The New York Girl is quick, chic, raven-shocked,
a now-and-then ache in the hearthstrings, a part
of the family. She stays. Others drop in, leave,
a murder film unwinds. Somebody has been killed,
the money is the clue, we smash everything apart
including the theater seats. A braying guides us
to the hanged donkey---eeyore! The suspect calls
New York, selecting a rare topaz for his escape.
He has murdered, feigned a drowning, gotten away
with it. We ride out into the country, but where
is the New York Girl? Not around anymore. We ask
about her, or others do. She was a little gaudy,
a little fast, a little fat. She went on a visit
to New York and when she started back on impulse
took a different train and went out of our lives
forever. What did you think of her, nuncle? "Oh,
I can't say. A New York Girl. She didn't fit in.
Of course [slight lift of the brow here] you had
a certain interest. It's normal. She's gone now,
the New York Girl." Ah, but I loved her, nuncle,
above life or licorice allsorts. I stayed quiet,
never told it, so our lives could go on, but oh!
I loved her like my own eye, that New York Girl.
And going home now, I try to phone but the phone
won't work---it spits ads instead of dial tones.
I drop it, by Wagner's Grocery, and start to run
down 10th Street to tag home before the intruder
from the garden breaks in, and I make it in time
to save everyone, but the New York Girl is gone.

ALL THAT DIVIDES

All that divides our houses
comes to less
than four fathoms of air.
Easy to wipe it out
and start over. Let's call
this gully full of garages
a lake. I am casting off now
and starting to row across.
You can hear the oarlocks
grumbling to themselves,
and the oar drops breaking
the water's vow of silence.
Open your dark-lantern
to lead me in. We'll watch
the watery stars
go up their ladders
into the old moon.

IN THE MALL

A friend snapped us
in a mall and years later
sent us the photo. We sit
a marital distance apart
on a slatted bench, reading.
But the unseen camera
has stolen our souls,
for on the wall behind us
a painted boy and girl rise
like our younger angels.
Your go-to-hell hat has a brim
pinned back like Leo Gorcey's
above a cock-eyed smile.
I steam briskly ahead
under a full head of hair.
We look twelve or thirteen.

Below, our astounded selves
read on, not noticing
that these two have left us
and are strolling off
to a different life. I hope
they'll be happy there—
at least, I finally see,
they are holding hands.

GODDESS & MUSE

Katherine, my colleague
    in the reading, is tall
        and honey-combed—

a kind intelligence. We talk
    of work, the small turnout,
        the difficulties of poems.

For a moment she lounges
    within her clothes,
        hips, belly hammocked,

and I, old man, am foolishly on fire
    for this beauty, for Ceres
        strewing the granary floor

with corn and flowers.
    Today the Muse passed me
        on Third Street. We spoke

and walked on. I turned
    to watch her out of sight.
        Some might have seen

a student, thin in jeans.
    But, old belovéd,
        I knew who you were.

LINES FOR A LUMINOUS DIAL

Small crystal light,
attend me through the dark—
time's vast unknowable,
your minute spark.

INVITATION TO A GHOST
(Written at my uncle's old typewriter)

Suppose you were to come back as a ghost,
where would you be most apt to hang around?
Those shelves of books you left me in your will
or maybe this clanking Remington machine
where you typed out the last day of your life?
I'm not an adept at this astral guff

and also know that you'd agree it's guff
and snort at the idea of something ghost-
written. A wraith who came around
would have to have more than a phantom will—
be more than just a ghost in the machine—
to punch these heavy characters to life.

But if you want a second shot at life,
don't think that I will give you any guff.
Take over. I'll go out and watch the ghost
of snow come through the willow. There's a round
carol of birdsong at the feeder. I'll
listen to that and wait for the machine

to stop. Maybe I'll go out and machine
a special key for ectoplasmic life
(this is what Hitchcock nicknamed a MacGuffin,
like finding a radio for ghost-to-ghost
communication). If I turned around
would you be scowling? I don't think I will

for fear I'd hear you say, "For God's sake, Will,
don't turn my mill into a pun machine,
or I'll come stalking right back into life
and put a stop to all this silly guff.
We've organized here for the right of ghosts
not to be made fun of or pushed around."

Pardon your namesake if he fools around.
It's just that, if I had a way to will
you back to write—a *deus ex machina*—
or chide the *Times* on spelling (in your life,
uncompromising as old Will McGuffey),
I'd call you a most welcome kind of ghost

and hope that ghost would always be around
and with a will return you your machine
to say the afterlife was not all guff.

DESCARTES AND THE ANGEL
(For friends in England)

Your medieval Christmas angel flew
its peacock splendors into the study where
Descartes was lying open on a chair,
part of the preparation for a new

semester. This was a red-haired angel of peace,
one wing toward Heaven, the other slanting down,
and wearing a most amazingly red gown
arranged into fantastic geometries.

It couldn't have begun to get into the air
(Cartesian logic demands separation
of intellect and imagination),
but here it was, just in from Lincolnshire.

A week late, it's true, and it had lost
its halo somewhere over the Atlantic
but for all that didn't appear frantic
at having fallen from the heavenly host.

I needed to think this over and went out
to take a walk, remembering that Descartes
cared not a bit for poetry or art
but left his study daily to go about

in anonymity among the Dutch.
This was in Amsterdam about the time
his townsman, Rembrandt Harmenszoon van Rijn,
was putting some of them into *The Night Watch*,

so that there must have been somewhere a face
common to the thinker's and the artist's eye,
by mind and heart considered equally,
and for at least a moment have been grace.
I close the book. Your angel holds the place.

SILKBY TO KELBY

The green-road runs
between fields
to a cross
with a sign tilting
toward Kelby church.

A pony turns
curiously
from the mounds
of a shrunken
medieval village,

Silkby. Gas guns
fire randomly
over the valley,
scaring the crows,
a lazy war.

One can walk
from Silkby to Kelby
in an hour
and see no one,
be seen by no one.

If not for the pony,
this borrowed coat
could as well
hang on its hook
as go empty here.

VI

IV

NOTES FROM THE ISLAND

Limited Knowledge

After 2,000 years, you dig
deeper to find less
of the shepherd and his wife—
a handstone he may have used,
some fragments
of the pot she made,
pressing triangles
into its braided band.
Perhaps she broke the pot,
or it sat here
until the roof fell.
Perhaps it held grain.
Perhaps they ran and hid
in the scree hole, where pirates
killed them.
Perhaps the pot was what
they couldn't carry
when they left
a relentless country
where nothing but stone
could stay.

Dear Whoever

The St. Kilda mailboat
sank.
By now, fish eyes are reading

my message to you,
fish lips are kissing
your name.
It's just the latest
mistake in communication.
The carrier pigeons crashed.
The spy swallowed my letter
with cyanide
and revealed nothing.
Writing in Urdu
was not a good idea.

Redefining Sheep

Soay sheep
are unmanaged,
unmanageable,
free as lions
in Africa.

No fat sheep
of the feeding floor,
bred to be docile,
to be silly
as sheep.

Archaic sheep
of the cave paintings,

dawn sheep
curious and nimble
as deer.

Noble tup
of the morning skyline,
horns curled,
nose up
for love
or danger,

reigning over
your own island
that bears
your fine
Norse name.

I write you
new similies—
brown as fleece,
carkled as wool,
smart, fleet,
subtle
as a sheep.

Leaving St. Kilda

There is no saint,
there is no island.

Hesperides, Hebrides.
Behind us,
the doors of the sea
are closing over Skildar,

which has
no saint at all, only
a name the Norse left
for barrier, shield,

which is not
one island even,
only a cloaking name
for many islands.

The boat moves
in the sun's power.
Skildar's old poets
sleep under Oiseval.

The ocean quiets
and weaves
with little winds
a winding of black linen.

Dead men fall down
into the sleep-nets
of the woven sea.
. . . .

The boat bears us
from dream to dream,
turning us
to the world.

There is no saint,
there is no island.

UNTITLED

oh that morning
when out window
sun banged broke
on days child dazed
bright whirring spoke
smoke of daybreak
smelt grass wet
green to skin
set eyewheels
spinning in lights
terror joy never
to be forgotten
the livelong dark.

RED GLADS, BLUE MOUNTAIN

All day the flower and painting
have accompanied each other
beside my desk, recalling Tozan's words,
how cloud and mountain are son
and father, how they rely
on each other in perfect freedom.
Without the mountain, the flowers
would pass unnoticed,
because of the flowers I see the fall
of water, and the lone boatman lowers
his line again into the abyss.

PONIES

Almost you can see
the dust they raise,
this little remuda
wheeling at a sound
to the far fence,
then cantering back—
almost, but they're
boys, not horses.
It's the way
their legs move
that catches me,
like film slowing
a stampede to one
long flowing motion,
and the whole day
in the way they go
down the street,
so beautiful
they don't even know.

LETTER FROM INDIANA

Susanna, I can't tell you why
the magic happens one night
and not another, so instead
I'll tell you about my friend Henry,
bedfast forty years in the county home,
who wrote ten thousand lines extolling
George Rogers Clark in heroic couplets,
unread, uncelebrated, and in sober fact
pretty punk,
but just as *there*, by God, as Xenophon.
And Rafinesque inventing the *Walum Olum*,
with pictographs to prove the Lenni Lenape
came from Siberia to Crawfordsville.
And my brother-in-law's
delirious buddies who fell
for inspired fakery in a Hoosier cave
and wrote a book to tell the delighted world
how Egyptians discovered Indiana.
We just keep hitting that old piñata,
hoping a blue eyeball will fall at our feet
and we'll pick it up, pocket it,
and walk off whistling, right past
the guards and into the green fields
of the Holy Ghost.

BERLIN REVISITED

At a table
outside the Konditorei
this Sunday morning,
sparrows pecking
under my feet, a song
running through my head.

> *With a love that's true,*
> *Sunday, Monday, or always.*

Berlin wakes up early
even on Sunday.
A church committee
is hanging greens
for a First Communion.
"Guten Morgen!"
a woman greets me,
emphatically.
An old man is out
buying bread. Women
are walking dogs
past a Kinderspielplatz,
green jungle world
between buildings—
how Europe manages

somehow to make
its cities human.

With a love that's true

Can't get that scrap
out of my head.
Who, what was loved,
Berlin, so long ago
before the Wall,
the Reichstag still
a burnt-out shell?
Divided heart, divided city.
All that gone now,
resolved finally
in spring sunshine,
one city again,
and the heart healed
(annealed at least),
though faces linger
and names kept somewhere
for forty years.
What's left is song,
simple as sun
after showers,
a sparrow tune.

I'll be loving you,
with a love that's true,
Sunday, Monday, or always

NEAR GOSHEN

Amish carriages plod the edge
of the road, like oldstyle thoughts
at the edge of the mind.
"Plod" is relative; in truth
the little horses step out briskly,
drawing their closed systems
like black and polished cupboards
industriously toward destinations
of farmhouse and family.
We imagine drivers harried
by traffic, endangered even,
but there is no haste in their faces,
no fear. In the other lane,
we think we are passing them,
but they have already passed us,
altering our plans like the slight pull
of dark companion stars.

SOME DREAMS

Some dreams we want
to return to, they had so much
to tell us, such deep resonance—
the woman in that house
of thoughtful objects
who was frail and wise,
and how we walked later
along a shaded street
and I picked up a stone
for memory.
That sleep was real.
Awake, I tried to find
my way back, but I'd lost
the directions, my stone.

AN IMPERFECT SONNET

The clerk slaps a stamp
on my letter to you,
obliquely. I want to say,
"Oh, take care. Let everything
today be perfect—your eyes,
sun catching lights
in your dark hair,
your private smile."
It is not so,
and I know it.
The letter travels
crookedly as the stamp,
a zig-zag path
through tumbling skies.

Take my words, dearest,
not for what they say
but what they would,
were I perfection's child
and this a perfect world.

MARTIAN MOMENT

We hold hands and gaze at the image
of Mars, which is streaking
nearer tonight than since the last Ice Age,
galactically speaking.

Thirty-five million miles or less—
no hot kiss exactly,
but not to be taken, we suggest,
too matter-of-factly.

Go for it, you guys, Mars and Earth!
Oppose intimately!
We know something, for what it's worth,
of apo- and perigee.

PYRUS COMMUNIS
(with a concluding line from W.S. Graham)

In Penticton, the wineries ran out
of pear wine, but our tree here
staggers with fruit, inexplicably.
We never saw blooms, and this tree
has seen hard times. Four years ago
an utter breakdown, the crop too thick.
A tree surgeon chopped everything.
The next year nothing, and the following,
then sudden wealth. We'll have
pear jam, butter, pie, pear wine
(if I can make it).

Why pears? I could say,
"My Aunt Laura Vandivier had a tree . . . ,"
or tell about the pears from Oregon
we scooped like ice cream,
or ring the names: Bosc, Bartlett,
Kieffer, Flemish Beauty, not forgetting
Seckel or sugar pear, Starking Delicious,
the Red Anjou, and, farther back, odd strains:
Crassane and Jargonelle. At home
Pear Orchard's children, too poor
for shoes, ran barefoot through spring snow.

"Pear, or its equivalent, occurs
in every Celtic language." Even its pests
are pear-shaped, mellifluous:
fire blight, pearl oyster scale, the pear midge.
Much like the apple (*P. malus*) but without
the bad rap, *communis*, a mellow friend.
Yet something more—a French orchard
espaliered, the antique yellow
fruit of troubadours and lovers,
tapestried. Graham sang it in a line:
"My heart is headhung on a peartree girl."

A MOUNTAIN THINKS

A mountain's thought takes a millennium,
    any little stone can do it faster.
    Its word is rock.

Plenty of time, it says, don't rush me.
    Come back next century. Maybe
    I'll have the answer.

A million years of sunrises may train
    a mountain's neurons to respond.
    Oh, hello. You again?

The mountain's a wet-plate photographer.
    In its quickest exposure,
    you won't be a blur.

Cities? What were they? I didn't notice.
    It takes more time than they had
    to impress me.

Grandeur, it says, you can have it,
    if that's what you want.
    I wouldn't know.

Worship, it says, I've heard that word,
    but it never moved me.
    It was their idea.

ALL-POINTS BULLETIN

You can be walking along,
writing a novel, when suddenly
you're deep in someone else's,

a cell-phone saga with kids amok,
philandering spouse, and where to get
broccoli or erotic massage.

No more point-to-point messages,
it's all widecasting now, everyone
sending like radio stars.

"I told him, don't go to Moldova,"
the girl said, walking by. I wanted
to write the ending to that story.

SALVATION
(Written for *Poets Against the War*)

In the village that was destroyed
to save it, the jungle
has come back. Small animals scurry
under the wasted moon.
It is safe now.

All the villages, the cities,
will be destroyed to save them.
Many things will be saved.

The child on the road
will be saved in an instant,
with the farmer's cow and his wife
drawing water.

The man looking up at the light
will be saved to a burnt shadow.

Whole nations will see
their salvation falling
like volcanic rain.

The terrorist will be saved
and the suicide bomber, the fisherman also
in the boiling sea.

The trees will be saved
and the long grass no longer
fear the wind.

Language will be saved.
We will understand finally
that war is peace, and that peace
had to be saved.

EPITHALAMIUM
(For Richard and Jennifer Walters Hamilton)

A wind off Cape St. Mary's caught the word
and passed it to a wave: "There are these two
who need to meet." The gruff St. Lawrence heard
and rumbled to Quebec. Ontario
told Manitoba, and the rumour spread
along the wheat fields to Saskatchewan.
A mountain in Alberta raised its head
to tell Columbia, "The match is on."

What rivers, seas, and provinces approved
can we do less today than ratify,
a cloud of witnesses to the power of love,
that laughs at distance and geography?
Of friendship, too, that touches common clay
with fire not altogether undivine
and can, on the most ordinary day,
turn Cana's water into comet wine.

Here in this place of compasses and charts
you bless us by a latitude of love
that draws into the compass of two hearts
our own dear journeys. May the One who moves
the stars and tides attend you on your way,
bless and beguile your lives that here are blent,
and bring us all, in fullness of our days,
to continents of blessing and content.

MACROMICROCOSMIC

"The Hubble telescope has found 1,500 to 2,000 new galaxies in an arc of sky no wider than a grain of sand held at arm's length. . . . Meanwhile, astronomers say two planets possibly capable of supporting life are circling a star in the Big Dipper." — Evening news

How apt to juxtapose
such twin immensities
at arm's length from the nose.

It's tempting to suspect
in sand and galaxies
some playful intellect

who dropped us in the middle
with both ends out of sight,
then went away to fiddle.

What anthropocentricity!
Meanwhile, the news tonight
reports with specificity

new planets have been found
like ours (almost). No doubt
we should get off the ground

and see if folk are sager
and have it figured out
by now, on Ursa Major.

YOUR BENCH

We've put it under the willow
where you can see out
without being seen.
It's like peering through
a beaded curtain or
in the attic a little window
only you know is there.
Be very quiet, listen,
you can hear a pear ripening
next door. A rabbit
lopes toward you but stops
to nibble violets. Even the sun
thinks you're somewhere else.

A NOTE (AND NOTES) ON THE POEMS

Poetry broke into my life in 1974 after a visit to Venice, and that life has never been the same since. In chapbooks, I tried to enforce some unity of theme. In this 30-year selection, it has seemed better to arrange poems by time, although not slavishly, and from this a different kind of pattern emerges. I see more clearly now what I was learning and doing in the 1970s and early '80s.

Poetry languished in the mid-'80s, and when it returned there was a revived interest in the art of it, applied to subjects of ordinary life. Sections II and III represent this and carry, I think, a sense of being written *in media res,* as in fact they were. I have never wanted to separate poetry from life or invest it with mist or mysticism. As various poets have said, poems are made with words.

My life took a sharp turn in the early 1990s when I lived and worked in the Far East for more than a year. Other travels followed, and Section IV opens out into a wider field of thought and observation. By the mid-1990s, I was back home, and the poems in Section V bring that wider perspective to a life of work, family, and friends.

The final section has a somewhat lighter touch (except in an instance or two), and draws on some themes of earlier years: travel, family, the nature of love and friendship, and the writer's art. Even as I say this, though, I'm aware of suggesting more pattern than may really be there. At any rate, poems must stand or fall on their own, not on the writer's life. None of the ones in this book really requires a note, but on the next page are a few explanations to help any curious or puzzled readers.

I thank Michael and Margaret Snow, literary executors of W.S. Graham, for allowing me to use the Graham line on Page 139. Finally, I owe a special debt to Mike O'Connor, a fine poet and translator of T'ang Dynasty poetry, who read and commented on the manuscript.

Page 26: "Hardtack's Verandah" was pictured in a photograph formerly in the Johnson County (Indiana) Historical Museum. "Hardtack" was a Johnson Countian of the early 20th Century (real name, Ebenezer Harbert). He also published poetry in the local newspaper, including "The Glories of Old Johnson" for which he won a 1906 "poetical contest." I am pleased to remember him here.

Page 30: Charles A. Vanderhoof was an American artist and illustrator of the late 19th and early 20th Century.

Page 80: Niyamóyoana Yabai's house is in Taiwan's aboriginal culture park near Sun-Moon Lake.

Page 97: Hellabrun is the Munich city zoo.

Page 113: "The New York Girl" is an attempt to impose a certain form by writing exactly equal lines on a manual typewriter, without proportional spacing. It records a dream.

Page 123: These poems are from a pamphlet, "Notes from the Island," written after taking part in a 2000 archaeological dig on the remote Scottish island of St. Kilda, often called "the island at the edge of the world."

Page 132: The writer was a young UPI reporter in Berlin about 1960 and more than 40 years later returned as an escort for students.

Page 144: "Epithalamium" was written for the wedding of friends in the Vancouver Maritime Museum—the bride from Newfoundland and the groom from British Columbia.

This book is typeset in a computer version of the famed Garamond typeface. The book was designed and formatted in MS Word by the author.

www.ingramcontent.com/pod-product-compliance
Lightning Source LLC
Chambersburg PA
CBHW031643040426
42453CB00006B/194